More Praise for *Jesus, The Ultimate Therapist: Bringing Hope and Healing*

"Dr. McAvoy's lessons are brief and inviting—not overwhelming for those with very full schedules! But what makes this guide exceptional is that we are encouraged not only to study about Jesus, but to "sit on the couch with Jesus" where in sharing our questions, fears, and challenges, we develop a precious intimacy with our Lord."

—Shirley Pieters Vogel, Author
wHispers: when He is so precious even rocks sing
New England Book Festival Winner, 2009

"Dr. McAvoy is clear about her identity as a psychotherapist and a person who has a personal relationship with Christ. In this study guide she does an excellent job of integrating these two.

The materials are clearly presented, encourage personal reflection on how faith is experienced in daily life, and offer a path to hope and healing."

—Duane A. Visser, MDiv, MC, retired Pastor /Chaplain
Christian Reformed Church

"This book is an excellent tool for pastors, small group leaders and all types of church leaders who would like to provide an extra level of pastoral care. The brief opening thoughts are calming and provide insightful and professional insights. The questions, added music suggestions, and Bible references make additional support available. I highly recommend this devotional."

—Sam Huizenga, Small Group Ministry Developer
Christian Reformed Home Missions

"Dr. McAvoy has put together this simple, yet wonderful devotional study that is grounded in Scripture. The daily readings lead one to seek the reality of Christ's provision and ministry to our personal lives. I found myself reflecting deeply and honestly about my own heart, brokenness, and need for Jesus to minister to me."

—Dan Rudman, MA, Evangelist
Ambassador's for Christ International-U.S.A.

Jesus,
The Ultimate Therapist

BRINGING HOPE AND HEALING

KERRY KERR MCAVOY, PhD

ISBN 13: 978-0-9843205-0-9

Scripture quotations identified (NIV) are taken from the HOLY BIBLE, NEW INTERNATIONAL VERSION®. NIV®. Copyright© 1973, 1978, 1984 by International Bible Society. Used by permission of Zondervan. All rights reserved.

Cover Designed by Lori Vezina
Printed in the United States of America

CONTENT

Acknowledgments

This book began as a dream and a hope in 2006. Many people have been instrumental in its development. I want to thank those who have supported me in this endeavor.

- Dr. Dennis Hensley for his patient editing, honest criticism, and helpful support.

- Barb DeKoekkoek and Sam Huizenga for their prayer support.

- Linda Kinney for her wonderful proofing services and encouragement.

- Lori Vezina for her fantastic book cover and interior layout.

- My parents, Larry and Valerie Kerr, for their faith and belief. As a young child, they told me I could do anything I wanted to once I set my mind to it.

- My sister, Karmen Kerr, for being my friend. She has been my personal cheerleader throughout this project.

- My sister, Kristin King, for her encouragement and quiet support.

- My husband, Brad, and sons, Cameron, Devon, and Kellin, who were my first readers. They believed I could do this and encouraged me every step of the way.

- And finally, Jesus, my sweet Savior, Teacher, and Friend. He woke me up with a dream and faithfully provided me with the necessary love, support, and encouragement throughout the entire process.

Introduction

E very new client seeking counseling comes into my office looking for a good therapist. The first few sessions set the framework for building a relationship of trust and support. The client is distressed and needing answers. Many different issues are discussed, and symptoms of anxiety and depression are often present. He or she may want help with difficult relationships. The person may be struggling with parenting issues and worrying about his or her children. Feelings of desperation and helplessness are common. Through successful psychological treatment, emotional reactions are processed, creative solutions are considered and implemented, and therapy terminates with the client healthier than when he or she came to the first appointment.

I frequently get asked how the counseling relationship is different from a good friendship. Is the main purpose of treatment to find solutions to client difficulties? And, finally, I am asked why "self-help" books often don't work.

The therapist-client relationship is an unusual one. It allows clients to be themselves without criticism or judgment. It is one-sided by nature, in that the therapist doesn't use the relationship to meet his or her emotional and social needs. Instead, the therapist's task is to provide the kind of environment that assists clients to address their neglected psychological needs and encourages their real selves to emerge.[1] It is through the safety of this psychological relationship that healing occurs.

Research consistently confirms that the relationship between therapist and client is the key to healing.[2] In fact, it is the main reason counseling is effective. The personal characteristics of therapists create a sense of safety and support that enables therapy to work. Therapists who are (1) empathetic, (2) honest and genuine, and (3) see their client's personal value and worth, are the most effective.[3] There is one problem. Good therapists are only human, and therefore prone to illness, boredom, and misunderstandings. At best, they can only achieve being good enough for their clients. Thankfully, this is often enough for treatment success.

Jesus, however, is the ultimate therapist. He embodies every characteristic that research identifies as qualities of a good counselor. We need a counselor who empathizes with our struggles. Jesus perfectly understands us and longs to meet our needs. He has faced every temptation. He has been misunderstood, persecuted, tortured, and crucified so that we can have a relationship with him. Jesus has been tempted in every way and sympathizes with our weaknesses (Hebrews 4:15).

Additionally, we need a therapist who is transparent. Jesus is completely open and honest. He doesn't manipulate, distort the truth, or use people. He is so open that he enraged those in power. We see this honesty in his conversation with the rich young man who was seeking the answer to inheriting eternal life. Jesus frankly confronted the question and disappointed the man (Mark 10:21–22).

Finally, we need a counselor who sees our personal value. Jesus' love for us is so deep that there is nothing we can do that would prevent him from longing to have a relationship with us. Paul recorded that "while we were still sinners, Christ died for us" (Romans 5:8). We can find no more effective counselor than Jesus. Complete understanding and healing can only be found in him.

It is enough that Jesus embodies all these excellent therapist qualities, but these characteristics are only the start. Jesus brings even more to his relationships. The psalmist has stated that Jesus contains everything one needs (paraphrase of Psalm 23:1). Relationship with him contains all that is necessary for healing, fulfillment, and wholeness. This devotional will explore the competency and sufficiency of Jesus through six specific roles he has with each person. It will delve into his ability to empathize, value and love every person. There is no other place for complete healing than Jesus Christ.

Comments on the Devotional

I am a clinical psychologist, not a theologian. You will notice that I include many questions. Socrates said to "know thyself." I find that real change comes only after increased self-awareness. For example, how can one stop drinking alcohol if he or she doesn't see the damage caused by the behavior? It is only after seeing the problem that one can do something about it. I believe this also applies to our spiritual life. Who is God really to me? What do I think and believe about him? When do I call on him for help, and why? By understanding the answers to these types of questions, I can see how I actually relate to Jesus, and I can measure the overall richness of this relationship and the degree to which it agrees with Scripture.

This devotional includes nontraditional questions. They are designed to focus on the health of your current relationship with Jesus. The goal of this study will be to grow in the understanding of God's desire for you. I long for you to be overwhelmed by this desire. God yearns for you. You are of great value to him, not because of what you can offer, but for who you are—regardless of beauty, age, or social status. Your value does not change despite your changing circumstances. You are and always will be precious to him.

I hope you don't just read the material, but also will interact with it. Here are suggestions to aid in that process. In this book there are six chapters. It is my intention that each chapter be a week-long focus. You will notice that each chapter starts out with a Key Scripture. This verse is to set the tone for the week. You may want to do some memorization work. This verse might fit that purpose well.

At the end of each day's entry there are questions. These are to facilitate your thinking. I encourage you to let the material work in your heart. The questions are just a start. I hope you will go further. Such as, do you agree or disagree with the readings? What is new? What is startling? How do the Scripture readings affect you? You may find yourself having a negative reaction. This is okay. God is not intimidated by our disagreements or frustrations with him.

Whether positive or negative, all reactions, with the exception of apathy or indifference, are relational. God loves us to struggle with him. Remember Jacob wrestling with God? The questions at the end of each day's reading are to start the process of your struggle with the material. Therapy is just like this struggle. Your counselor makes an observation about something you do. You need to test this observation. Is it true, and under what circumstances? Of course, the Bible is accurate, but do you behave as if it is? Why or why not? Let the questions take you further in your relationship with Jesus. Let it lead you to new places with him.

You may find that you will want to keep a companion journal for note taking. I know some of us love to use writing as a way to process our reactions and emotions. Some ideas for the use of a journal are: to note other Bible passages or stories that come to your mind as you work through each chapter; to journal your reaction to the study material; or to note songs and events to illuminate where you are with Jesus at that moment.

I have included a meditation exercise for each chapter. As I mentioned before, it is my desire that we will develop a personal experience with Jesus. Too much of our spiritual life can be about praying to Jesus or focusing on our knowledge of Jesus without really being *with* Jesus. To be in relationship with someone means there is a give and take or mutuality. We need to spend time just "being" with Jesus and "listening" to him. The meditation exercises are designed to help facilitate the listening part of our relationship with him.

Finally, you will find a musical playlist of songs at the end of each chapter. I have included them to give you another way to spend time with Jesus. Music brings something unique to my life with Jesus. I worship easier with music. Sometimes a song will illuminate a different thought or idea about God. My playlist is by no means exhaustive or complete. It is just a start. You may have your favorites that capture the spirit of any given chapter. But I hope my song suggestions will add another dimension to your time with Jesus as you work through this devotional.

So, with all of that said, let's sit on the couch with Jesus, the ultimate therapist!

Chapter 1

Emmanuel

KEY SCRIPTURE

"The virgin will be with child and will give birth to a son, and they will call him Immanuel—which means, 'God with us.'"

Matthew 1:23

Each of us has core physical needs, such as food, rest, and shelter. Without these essentials we would die. Just as there are basic physical needs, there are also core emotional needs. One of these emotional requirements is our need to be in community. In other words, we need to be with people who know and care about us. This psychological drive causes us to fear being abandoned and to avoid being rejected. Most of us dislike and evade complete social isolation. I often hear clients dreading the sense of being on their own without someone to love them. We will do almost anything to avoid such seclusion.

This need is not just an emotional one; it is also a spiritual one. God understands this and has sent us Jesus. He is "Emmanuel" or *God with us.* Jesus is the human example of God who wants to live with and relate to us.

Many years ago I heard Paul Harvey's annual radio broadcast Christmas story that clarifies this.[4] I will attempt to retell it in my own words. There was a farmer who watched the weather worsen as a winter storm approached. He saw the birds flutter around, looking for a warm place to roost and escape the harsh cold winds. He quickly walked outdoors and threw open the doors of his warm barn, sprinkling bird seed on the floor. Despite the attractive warmth of the barn, the birds did not fly in. The farmer tried shooing them in, but that only frightened them further. Finally, he mumbled to himself, "If only I could become like a bird and fly in ahead of them to show them the way to safety." Paul Harvey finished this tale by drawing the conclusion that God came in the form of Jesus to be with us and to show us the way to a fulfilled life, rich with meaning and love.

What a powerful message. God understands that I cannot be on my own. Jesus has come. His spirit lives within my heart. I matter to God so much that he sent his only son, Jesus, so I can know him. No matter my life circumstance, I am never alone. Jesus is my Emmanuel!

OPENING QUESTIONS

Have you experienced a long period of loneliness?

How did you deal with it?

How have you seen yourself and others avoid social isolation?

In what ways do you need to see more of Jesus as Emmanuel in your life?

MEDITATION EXERCISE

God is continuously speaking to us and wants to address us. This week look at the beauty in nature around you. Let what you see be a personal message from God to you. Record what you hear God saying to you in your journal, or share it with someone else.

PLAYLIST

"You're Here"
You're Here Francesca Battistelli

"Our Hope Endures"

Relentless Natalie Grant

"How Great is our God"

Arriving Chris Tomlin

"You Are God Alone"

Let the Worshippers Arise Phillips, Craig & Dean

God is With Me

KEY READING

Keep your lives free from the love of money and be content with what you have, because God has said,

"Never will I leave you;
never will I forsake you."

So we say with confidence,

"The Lord is my helper; I will not be afraid.
What can mere mortals do to me?"

Hebrews 13:5–6

It is not uncommon to have new clients come into my office and begin to tell me of their recent life difficulties. Usually, these individuals are resourceful and have tried many different solutions to their problems, but nothing seems to help. By the time they reach my office they are exhausted and weary. Often they are losing hope. It is at this point they feel all have abandoned them: their families, friends, and even God. Maybe you have experienced such a psychological space. I know I have. But is this feeling accurate?

God promises to be with us. All through the Old and New Testaments he reminds us of this truth. I know one of my greatest fears is that I will be all alone. This feeling is at its strongest when all seems to be going wrong and I feel helpless. God not only knows this fear, but understands it at its deepest level. "Who shall separate us from the love of Christ?" Romans 8:35 boldly declares. Paul continues in Romans 8:32–39 to outline some dramatic circumstances that challenge or shake most of us to the core: death, demons, our present situations, the unknown future. Yet, he concludes that Christ's love will prevail. No matter what comes my way, God will be with me and I will not be alone.

❧ What types of circumstances challenge your relationship with God?

❧ Which of today's key or optional verses seem to be the hardest to believe and depend on?

❧ What gets in the way of your confidence with the truth in the Key Reading?

❧ How is God speaking to you about his name Emmanuel through this verse?

❧ How will you use this new insight of Emmanuel as you face the situations and circumstances of your daily life and in life's hardships?

PRAYER

Lord, I confess that I have often felt alone when life's circumstances have been hard. I understand that you have promised never to leave nor forsake me. Please increase my faith and give me a greater sense of your presence and love as I face each day.

OPTIONAL READINGS

Exodus 3:11–12

Isaiah 43:2–7

Romans 8:22–39

God Longs to Relate to Us

KEY READING

Then the man and his wife heard the sound of the Lord God as he was walking in the garden in the cool of the day, and they hid from the Lord God among the trees of the garden. But the Lord God called to the man, "Where are you?"

Genesis 3:8–9

More than half of my counseling practice is about helping people deal with anxiety. It is the most commonly reported mental health complaint in this country.[5] Clients with this problem feel that life is unpredictable and fraught with danger. Their sense of control over themselves or life circumstances is tenuous and fragile. They often feel they are all alone. They struggle with believing God cares about them.

This belief is a lie. There is a continuing thread throughout the Bible. In fact, it is the whole point of the gospel: God's desire to relate to us. God longs "to be with us." We see this first when God walked in the garden with Adam in the cool of the evening. Then Adam and Eve fell and had to leave the perfection of the garden. Despite such disastrous outcomes and consequences, God was still there reaching out and making a way back to himself. We see this in Genesis 3 when God made garments of skin for Adam and Eve to clothe their shame. Then in Genesis 4, Eve gave birth to her first child, Cain. She saw God with her, despite her isolation from the former intimacy of the garden. She proclaimed, "With the help of the Lord I have brought forth a man" (Genesis 4:1). This story of reconciliation is repeated again and again, from Abraham to

Judah to Rahab to Joseph to Deborah to David to Solomon to Isaiah to Daniel to us.

God longs to be with us. Despite our life circumstances, we can be confident of this truth. Jesus is the culmination of this promise.

❦ What spoke to you in the key reading?

❦ Have you viewed God's relationship with the men and women of the Bible as a desire to relate to you? Why or why not?

❦ How does the revelation of "God's pursuit of you" change things?

PRAYER

Lord, thank you for your desire to have a personal relationship with me. I, too, want to have a deepening relationship with you. Please show me what keeps me from drawing closer to you.

OPTIONAL READINGS

Genesis 32:22–30

Exodus 3:2–5

1 Kings 19:10–13

Revelation 21:1–4

Emmanuel, Jesus is "God with Us"

KEY READING

The Son is the radiance of God's glory and the exact representation of his being, sustaining all things by his powerful word. After he had provided purification for sins, he sat down at the right hand of the Majesty in heaven.

Hebrews 1:3

Who really is Jesus? A prophet? A madman? Or who he says he is? He says he is God incarnate. Confusion around Jesus' identity has existed since the beginning. But who is Jesus to you? How would it change things if you could accept that Jesus is God? That is the critical question. Jesus cannot know you or affect your life if he is only a peripheral figure to you.

Clients are often referred to counseling by an outside source, such as their medical doctor or pastor. This can be problematic if the client doesn't see his or her need for therapy and is only complying with another's wishes. He or she is not truly motivated to address his or her problems. In such situations counseling is at risk of being a waste of time and of accomplishing little. Your spiritual life can have this same issue. You cannot be impacted by Jesus unless you accept that he is God.

The author in Hebrews says that Jesus is the "exact representation" of God. He is very specific in his definition of this. Hebrews 1:3 says Jesus is the exact representation of "his being." In other words, Jesus is the complete or full revelation of God. If you want to know God, then you can get no clearer picture of who God is than by looking at Jesus.

❧ How have you defined Jesus in the past?

❧ If you haven't seen him as the full revelation of God, how does this insight change things for you?

❧ Is there something you have read about Jesus that makes you struggle with him as the revelation of God?

PRAYER

Dear Jesus, thank you for coming and showing me God. Let this revelation that you are God with "flesh on" become more real to me. Let it change me and how I view you.

OPTIONAL READINGS

Isaiah 7:14

John 8:54–59; 10:30

Emmanuel, the Fulfillment of "God with Us"

KEY READING

Then I saw "a new heaven and a new earth," for the first heaven and the first earth had passed away, and there was no longer any sea. I saw the Holy City, the new Jerusalem, coming down out of heaven from God, prepared as a bride beautifully dressed for her husband. And I heard a loud voice from the throne saying, "Look! God's dwelling place is now among the people, and he will dwell with them. They will be his people, and God himself will be with them and be their God. "He will wipe every tear from their eyes. There will be no more death' or mourning or crying or pain, for the old order of things has passed away."

Revelation 21:1–4

Since the creation of the universe, God has longed to relate to us. He walked with Adam and Eve in the Garden of Eden until their disobedience separated them from him. This failure didn't discourage or stop God. The Old Testament is filled with stories of God making a way to connect to us only to have our sinfulness destroy his efforts. Then Jesus came as God in flesh to lead us back to God. He came in the form of a baby. He became approachable. His ministry yet today reaches out to the outcast, the unlovable, and the untouchable. He continues to welcome all, to know each person by name, and to heal.

God continually exerts great effort to maintain the connection between himself and us. The Bible speaks to this truth. Jesus once healed a lame man and then told the Jews around him who questioned his authority to perform a miracle on the Sabbath that "my Father is always at his work to this very day, and I, too, am working" (John 5:17). What was and is this work? It is to draw us to him so that Revelation 21 can be fulfilled—that God can make a comfortable dwelling with us all.

🌿 What has your relationship been like with God?

🌿 How does it impact you, knowing that God has made great efforts to relate to you?

🌿 How do you observe God showing up in your life to draw you to himself?

PRAYER

Dear Lord, thank you for caring so much for me that you go to such extremes to reach out to me. Thank you for sending your son Jesus so I can know you better. Help me to develop a closer relationship with you.

OPTIONAL READINGS

Genesis 3:8

Exodus 25:8

Luke 4:16–21

Concluding Thoughts

God understands our most basic needs, including our desire to be in relationships with others. In fact, this is a God-given desire; one that he has gone to great lengths to address. He has sent us Jesus, who is human, approachable, and "God in flesh." If we want our lives to be changed for the better, then the starting point is our acceptance that Jesus is God here with us. We are never alone. Jesus' last words as he ascended into heaven were, "I am with you always, to the very end of the age" (Matthew 28:20). We can trust in the presence of Jesus in all of life's circumstances.

Chapter 2

Word of God

KEY SCRIPTURE

"In the beginning was the Word, and the Word was with God, and the Word was God."

John 1:1

We therapists have one main tool that we use to help clients with their problems: our words. We generally don't touch, hug, or lay our hands on our clients. Unless we are psychiatrists, medical doctors with a specialty in psychiatry, we don't prescribe medication. Words are what we use to create a space for healing.

Words are powerful. The right word can create a connection with another person resulting in him or her feeling understood. It can illuminate a particular insight or chronic behavior pattern to a client. Wrong words can confuse and mislead. They can even cause discouragement. I remember hearing of a study where test subjects were repeatedly told by others that they looked ill. After hearing the same message again and again, the test subjects often began to feel ill, despite the fact that there was nothing wrong with them. Words are compelling and can create an emotional or possibly even a physical reality in the hearer.

It is interesting that "Word" is used to capture an essence of Jesus Christ. Why not soul? Or spirit? Or humanity? What is so important about Jesus being the Word of God? Let's explore these questions in the subsequent four devotionals.

OPENING QUESTIONS

Do you agree or disagree that words are powerful? Explain.

Think of a time when someone said something that strongly impacted you. How did it affect you?

What does it mean to you that Jesus is the Word of God?

What questions/issues do you have about this aspect of Christ?

BRINGING HOPE AND HEALING

MEDITATION EXERCISE

Lectio divina (Latin for "divine reading") is a traditional practice of Scripture reading and prayer. Choose a Scripture passage you would like to focus on this week. You may find a set of Bible verses in one of the "key or optional readings" from this chapter, or you may wish to choose one of your favorite passages. I recommend Colossians 1:15–20. Read it aloud, slowly, and with close attention. After the reading, ask God to speak to you through this passage. Re-read the passage aloud. Listen and journal (if you so choose) about what you hear God saying to you through these verses. You may want to use the same passage several days in a row. It is surprising to find that God has new things to say as you invest additional time into reading, mulling over and weighing the same passages.

PLAYLIST

"Conversation"

Conversation Sara Groves

"Creation Song"

The Breaking of the Dawn Fernando Ortega

"Sometimes Yes, Sometimes No"

Jill Paquette Jill Paquette

The Power of the Word

KEY READING

In the beginning was the Word, and the Word was with God, and the Word was God. He was with God in the beginning. Through him all things were made; without him nothing was made that has been made. In him was life, and that life was the light of all mankind.

John 1:1–4

What does it mean that Jesus is the Word of God? Both John and the author of Hebrews tell us that all things are created and sustained through Jesus. Jesus is the Word and it is by that word that the universe was spoken into existence and maintains stasis. God spoke and the physical realm was generated. Light separated from darkness, form from void, and water from dry land. All were separated by the action of God speaking.

This force goes beyond what we normally imagine when we think of words having power. As a therapist, I am aware of the power of my spoken words. Many times clients have told me how impactful some of my comments or observations have been. These words resonated with them and influenced their behaviors. This therapeutic power is nothing compared to Jesus' spoken word. Jesus isn't just influencing others; he is actually affecting the physical realm through his spoken word.

John tells us that through him (that is, Jesus) all things were made and without him nothing was made (John 1:3, author's paraphrase). Hebrews takes this even further by telling us that by the same "power words" all things are currently being sustained. The Word, spoken all those years ago to create the world, continues to sustain the universe. "The Son is the radiance of God's glory and the exact representation of his being, sustaining all things by his powerful word" (Hebrews 1:3). Jesus is the powerful, accomplishing Word of God.

❦ As you contemplate the key reading, what is new or different in your thinking about Jesus as the powerful Word of God?

❦ Have you thought of Jesus as being directly involved in the act of creating and sustaining you?

❦ How does this change your relationship with Jesus in light of him being the Word of God?

PRAYER

Dear Jesus, you being the Word God used to speak creation into existence is foreign to me. Forgive me for not seeing you as the powerful Word of God. Let your Word work powerfully in my life.

OPTIONAL READINGS

Genesis 1:1–3

John 3:33–35

Hebrews 1:2–3

Jesus, God's Spoken Word

KEY READING

Then Jesus cried out, "Whoever believes in me does not believe in me only, but in the one who sent me."

"For I did not speak on my own, but the Father who sent me commanded me to say all that I have spoken. I know that his command leads to eternal life. So whatever I say is just what the Father has told me to say."

John 12:44, 49–50

Jesus is not only the words God used to create the universe, but he is also the faithful communicator of God. When Jesus speaks, God is also speaking. Many have struggled with this aspect of Jesus. In fact, the New Testament frequently records that Jesus angered the crowds with his words. Can you imagine yourself listening to a charismatic teacher or speaker telling you mid-presentation that every word he is speaking is the literal word of God? I, like many of you, would probably think the speaker was crazy. But the Bible records over and again that we are hearing God speak when we listen to Jesus.

Jesus tells us in John 12:49 that he is faithful not only to the content of God's words, but also to the context. I find that very hopeful. Jesus gives messages of love, hope, and encouragement and does it in a consistent, gentle, patient way. He tells us that all this is a faithful representation of not just himself, but also of God. Remember the previous day's devotion that referenced Hebrews 1:3? Jesus is the *exact* representation of his (God's) being (my paraphrase and emphasis). Jesus is approachable because God longs to be approached. What we see and hear from Jesus is God's communication to us.

❦ Have you taken everything that Jesus said as being the literal words of God? If not, why not?

❦ How does it change your spiritual life to see Jesus as the exact representation of God's being?

❦ Have there been any words of Christ that you haven't wanted to accept as God's message to you? If so, what will you do with them now?

PRAYER

Dear Jesus, I confess I haven't always viewed you as God's spoken Word. I ask that you sensitize my "spiritual ears" to hear you. Let me be touched and moved by God's pursuing love as I listen to you.

OPTIONAL READINGS

John 1:14, 18

Philippians 1:12–18

1 John 2:22–23

Jesus Speaks Words of Life

KEY READING

As Jesus approached Jericho, a blind man was sitting by the roadside begging. When he heard the crowd going by, he asked what was happening. They told him, "Jesus of Nazareth is passing by."

He called out, "Jesus, Son of David, have mercy on me!"

Those who led the way rebuked him and told him to be quiet, but he shouted all the more, "Son of David, have mercy on me!"

Jesus stopped and ordered the man to be brought to him. When he came near, Jesus asked him, "What do you want me to do for you?"

"Lord, I want to see," he replied.

Jesus said to him, "Receive your sight; your faith has healed you." Immediately he received his sight and followed Jesus, praising God. When all the people saw it, they also praised God.

Luke 18:35–43

Jesus often performed miracles just by using his speech. His words contained authority. He didn't have to jump up and down or even raise his voice to the level of a shout. He spoke and the forces of nature obeyed. Here is a sampling of miracles to give us a sense of this authority:

- Healed demon possessed: Matthew 17:18; Mark 1:23–25; 5:6–13; 9:20–29.

- Cursed a fig tree: Matthew 21:18–19.

- Healed the sick: Mark 1:40–41; 3:5; 7:32–35; Luke 4:38–39; 5:12–13; 17:11–19; 18:35–43; John 5:1–9.

- Forgave a man his sin: Mark 2:3–11; John 8:1–11.
- Controlled the environment around himself: Mark 4:39; Luke 5:4–10; John 2:1–9; 21:5–6.
- Gave thanks and multiplied food: Mark 8:6–9; John 6:5–13.
- Resurrected the dead: Mark 5:35–43; Luke 7:11–15; John 11:17–44.

Over and again, Jesus used his "Word power" to bring healing and freedom into the lives of those around him. Today he longs to bring this same Word power into our lives.

✤ Are you surprised by the authority contained in the words of Jesus?

✤ What words of healing or freedom do you need Jesus to speak into your life?

✤ What stands in the way of you allowing Jesus to work in your life?

PRAYER

Dear Jesus, thank you for your wonderful words of life and freedom. Please work in my life with your healing words. Set me free from the fears that keep me from drawing closer to you.

OPTIONAL READINGS

Psalm 107:19–20

Luke 8:49–56

Jesus is the Living and Active Word of God

KEY READING

Do not merely listen to the word, and so deceive yourselves. Do what it says. Anyone who listens to the word but does not do what it says is like someone who looks at his face in a mirror and, after looking at himself, goes away and immediately forgets what he looks like. But whoever looks intently into the perfect law that gives freedom, and continues in it—not forgetting what they have heard, but doing it—they will be blessed in what they do.

James 1:22–25

Nothing is hidden from the Word of God. God sees and knows our internal struggles. He sees into the secret, dark places of our hearts. But this does not need to strike fear in us. God knows we are filled with doubts, fears, and even darkness. "But God demonstrates his own love for us in this: While we were still sinners, Christ died for us" (Romans 5:8). Everything has always been known to him; it is only ourselves that we are attempting to fool. Can I face the knowledge that I am broken and in need of God? Or will I keep trying to fix life's problems by myself? Jesus urges us with the words, "He who has ears to hear, let him hear." To *hear* the words of Jesus means to be transformed by them. They are powerful and life-changing. They are already spoken to each one of us. It is up to us to let the words of Jesus fill our lives and hearts. They will bring change and healing. Can we be honest with Christ and ourselves about our need so that we can be set free?

✻ Are there places within you that you have not faced and you've kept from God?

✻ What doubts or fears have been obstacles to letting God into those places?

✻ What will you do differently once you admit that God has always known your struggles and doubts, yet longs to work in your life?

PRAYER

Dear Jesus, you are the living and active Word of God who knows my thoughts and heart. Forgive me for trying to hide some of myself from you. Bring your words of love and life into all of me. I want to be healed and set free.

OPTIONAL READINGS

Hebrews 4:12–13

1 John 2:1–5

Concluding Thoughts

Words have tremendous power. They build up, encourage, isolate, influence, and even manipulate. For example, children ostracizing a fellow student can make him forever feel like an outsider or a misfit. Words have been used to sway crowds into following madmen and into doing terrible things for a cause. They have rallied people to perform heroic acts of bravery during times of crisis. Many things have been done simply through the influence of words.

Jesus' words are more than powerful. Jesus is the literal word of God. He was the power behind the act of creation and currently is sustaining the universe by his word. When he speaks, God is speaking. Jesus wants to bring this kind of victory and strength into our lives. He wants to heal and enrich our lives through his wonderful, living, active words.

Chapter 3

Light of God

KEY SCRIPTURE

"The Lord is my light and my salvation—whom shall I fear?"

Psalm 27:1

A female client sits in the chair across from me. She recently has developed several psychological symptoms. With some fear and reluctance, she has decided to seek help and now is in my office giving me the background to her condition. These emotional and physical ailments are uncomfortable and alarming. She feels out of control and doesn't recognize herself. She reacts differently to normal situations. She isn't sleeping well, and her appetite has changed. She has no idea what is going on.

Questions hang in the air during this initial interview. What is wrong? Have I, as the professional, seen this problem before? Will the treatment recommendations work? These are normal concerns of first-time counseling clients. I can see the expressions of relief on her face as I give a diagnosis and identify the treatment goals. I reassure her that this is a familiar problem and that it responds well to therapy. She leaves the appointment feeling a glimmer of hope and some encouragement. She is no longer in the dark about her illness.

We hate being in the dark, whether it is a physical darkness or an emotional one. We feel lost and vulnerable. We grope around with our hands trying to recognize previously familiar landmarks. Such a state makes God seem absent from us. How do we find him when we can't even find our way to the places we know?

Genesis tells us that the physical realm started out formless, empty, and dark (Genesis 1:2). But even in the darkness, God was still there. The Spirit of God was hovering over this emptiness. Then the first act of creation occurred: light. This wasn't the creation of the sun, moon or stars—all the things that we think of as light-creating in our lives. No, this was the presence of light. God created light. This was the first structure or form made out of the empty, black void. What was God saying by making this his very first creation?

Jesus is revealed as the Light of God. We do not need to fear the darkness. We have Christ who lights our path. He makes form out of the formless and dispels the darkness: physical, emotional, and spiritual. He is filled with light, yet is more than light. He comes to be a beacon of love, hope, and revelation in a world filled with great darkness.

OPENING QUESTIONS

When you think of Jesus as the Light of the World or Light of God, what comes to your mind?

BRINGING HOPE AND HEALING

How does it make you feel to think of Jesus this way?

In what ways do you need a greater experience of Jesus as the Light of God in your life?

MEDITATION EXERCISE

Richard Foster, in his book *Celebration of Discipline*, describes a meditation exercise called "palms down, palms up."[6] I am modifying it slightly to fit this study. Place your palms in your lap in the upright position as if to receive something. Identify the dark things in your life. It might be a worry, some interpersonal difficulty, a loss of some kind, or even a hurt within yourself. Imagine these things setting atop the palms of your hands. Now turn your palms downward. Imagine yourself letting them fall at the feet of Jesus and pray a releasing prayer. For example, "I release my fear of the upcoming medical test." After taking some time to surrender these areas of darkness, turn your palms upward. This time receive from God his light into these areas. "Lord, I receive your light and peace in the upcoming medical test." Spend several minutes in silence with your heart listening to what else God might be saying to you.

"Great Light of the World"

Myself When I Am Real Bebo Norman

"Be Thou My Vision"

Greatest Hymns Selah

"Light of the World"

A Grateful People Watermark

Jesus, the Promised Light

KEY READING

The sun will no more be your light by day,
   nor will the brightness of the moon shine on you,
for the Lord will be your everlasting light,
   and your God will be your glory.
Your sun will never set again,
   and your moon will wane no more;
the Lord will be your everlasting light,
   and your days of sorrow will end.

Isaiah 60:19–20

God created a perfect place, a garden for humanity. Yet, it was lost due to Adam and Eve's disobedience. The world became so distant and separated from God that he wiped out the human race with a flood and started over with Noah's family. Even this re-do didn't change things. Before long, the earth was dark with humanity's continued rejection of God. This time a promise was made to Abram. A blessing would come through Abraham's line. Jesus would lead everyone back to God. He would be a light that would bring life again to all people. Jesus was that promise. John points to him as a light to every person. This light illuminates the way back to God. It brings salvation to all the earth. It creates a world where all darkness is dispelled: death, disease, pain, violence, sin, and sorrow. Have I let the light shine into my darkness?

❧ Where do you need darkness dispelled in your life?

❦ Have you let Christ bring the light of salvation into your life?

❦ Do you hold on to the hope that all the darkness will someday come to an end? If not, why not?

PRAYER

Dear Jesus, thank you for being the promised light of the world. Please finish your work in bringing salvation to all the earth. Come light my life, inside and outside. Please light the dark corners of my heart.

OPTIONAL READINGS

Genesis 12:2–3

Isaiah 49:6

Jesus, the Light of Wisdom

KEY READING

Now the serpent was more crafty than any of the wild animals the Lord God had made. He said to the woman, "Did God really say, 'You must not eat from any tree in the garden'?"

The woman said to the serpent, "We may eat fruit from the trees in the garden, but God did say, 'You must not eat fruit from the tree that is in the middle of the garden, and you must not touch it, or you will die.'"

"You will not certainly die," the serpent said to the woman. "For God knows that when you eat from it your eyes will be opened, and you will be like God, knowing good and evil."

When the woman saw that the fruit of the tree was good for food and pleasing to the eye, and also desirable for gaining wisdom, she took some and ate it. She also gave some to her husband, who was with her, and he ate it. Then the eyes of both of them were opened, and they realized they were naked; so they sewed fig leaves together and made coverings for themselves.

Genesis 3:1–7

As Eve stood at the forbidden tree of knowledge of good and evil, she was longing to understand, to know, to be like God. This is a desire we understand. How many times have we drawn close to something that promised enlightenment, yet actually proved to be death and darkness wrapped up attractively? Eve had the opportunity to walk with and know God. She could have learned the secrets of the universe from the Creator of all things. Instead, she reached and took the fruit of death and separation from God.

Everyone is looking for personal fulfillment. Advertisements suggest that buying and using the right product will bring fame, popularity, or sex appeal. Women starve themselves to be beautiful. Men spend time and money pursuing the next thrill. The pitiful substitutes that the world offers, which bring nothing but pain and misery, are swapped for God's wisdom found in Jesus Christ.

Education is a large part of therapy. Counselors use their knowledge of psychological conditions, past clinical experiences, and personal intuition to teach clients. The reservoir of knowledge that therapists draw on is puny in comparison to Jesus' resources. He is the light of wisdom. If we want real peace regarding our doubts and questions, then we need go no further than Jesus for those answers. He longs to reveal the hidden things of God to us: that we are precious, loved, and claimed.

❧ Have you seen Jesus as the Light of Wisdom of God?

❧ When looking for answers, where do you tend to go for solutions? To a habit or an addiction? To others? To yourself?

❧ What would be different if you sought Jesus instead?

PRAYER

Dear Jesus, thank you for being the light of God's wisdom. I confess I usually don't see you that way. I have relied on my own strength or the wisdom of the world too much. Help me to turn to you for answers to my problems and struggles.

OPTIONAL READINGS

Daniel 2:20–23

1 Corinthians 1:18–25

2 Corinthians 4:6

Jesus, Our Guiding Light

KEY READING

When Jesus spoke again to the people, he said, "I am the light of the world. Whoever follows me will never walk in darkness, but will have the light of life."

John 8:12

One of the more frustrating experiences when we are in a strange place during a moonless night is to have our flashlight batteries die. Suddenly, we are plunged into complete darkness. Disoriented, we cautiously move forward only to trip on some rock or uneven ground.

How much of our lives are spent in a similar fashion? We live just trying to get by only to lose sight of our goals. Or we think we are moving forward, only to stop and check and find we haven't made any headway. Jesus knows our plight. God did not lead the Israelites out of Egypt only with a map, a nice slap on the back, and a wish of good luck. No, he was intimately involved in their deliverance. He came as a guiding light to lead the way to the Promised Land: cloud by day and pillar of fire by night (Exodus 13:20–22). God was patient in his provision of light. The two week journey took the Israelites forty years to finish, yet God continued to lead the way.

Jesus tells us that if we follow him, we will never walk in darkness again. We will never be lost or led astray. This promise doesn't stop here though, as wonderful as it is. Jesus takes it a step farther. He informs us his light will shine through us to a dark world around us. Those who are followers of Jesus' light can shine his light to those in the dark. Are we letting the light of Jesus shine?

❦ Are you trusting in Jesus to light your way? What does that mean practically?

❦ What was a recent experience of God's guiding light directing you?

❦ Are you shining the light of Jesus to the lost world around you? If so, how?

PRAYER

Dear Jesus, thank you for being my guiding light. I realize that I don't always look for your light as I walk life's journey. Forgive me when I stray from your lighted path. Help me follow you more closely. Help me let your light brighten my corner of the world.

OPTIONAL READINGS

Matthew 5:14–16

John 11:9–10

Ephesians 5:8–14

Jesus, the Light of Righteousness and Hope

KEY READING

For you were once darkness, but now you are light in the Lord. Live as children of light (for the fruit of the light consists in all goodness, righteousness and truth) and find out what pleases the Lord. Have nothing to do with the fruitless deeds of darkness, but rather expose them. It is shameful even to mention what the disobedient do in secret. But everything exposed by the light becomes visible—and everything that is illuminated becomes a light. This is why it is said:

"Wake up, sleeper,
*   rise from the dead,*
and Christ will shine on you."

Ephesians 5:8–14

Psychologists have been researching one of the great mysteries of human development: the formation of self-consciousness. How do we become distinct individuals with our own likes and dislikes when our physical structures are the same? We each have a brain that is comprised of neurons. Why are we different from one another? Although genetics plays a major role, it seems that our first relationships also are an important part in the development of our personality or "self." In other words, the way we experience our parents' care and love for us helps to shape our personality. If they consistently provide for our needs, we come to believe we are worthy of another's attention. If they praise us for our accomplishment, we learn that we can please others by our decisions and behaviors.

No parent is perfect, misunderstandings happen, and crises occur. People can get ill or die. A million things can go wrong despite good intentions. Personality insecurities can develop. It may seem as though I am blaming parents for psychological problems. I am not. I have seen clients overcome unbelievable losses and abuses. I also have seen other clients have severe psychological issues despite growing up in a relatively healthy family structure. There is much that psychology does not understand about personality development, but a primary relationship seems to play an important role in the shaping of our identity.

Jesus wants to be part of this modeling process. He longs to be our guiding light. Even under the best circumstances, parenting can go wrong. This isn't so with Jesus. He perfectly sees and knows every one of us. He empathizes with our plight. He yearns to show us who we are to him. He is never weary, bored, or frustrated with us. Jesus wants us to root ourselves in him. In his eyes, we are worthy, valued, and loved.

Jesus tells us that if we follow him, we will never walk in darkness again. We will never be lost or led astray. He tells us his light will shine into the darkest parts of ourselves. He will set us free from our doubts and will comfort us with his love. He calls to us to come out of our personal darkness to live in his righteousness and hope.

❧ What was one of the shaping moments you experienced as a child? Does it still affect you today? If so, how?

❧ Are there any continuing places of darkness in your life currently?

❧ How would you or your life change if you were to allow Jesus to expose where you need more of his love and guidance?

❧ What is getting in your way of doing that?

PRAYER

Dear Jesus, you are the light of righteousness and hope. Thank you for the joy you bring to my life. Cleanse any darkness in me, and lead me completely into your light. Help me to define myself by the way you see me.

OPTIONAL READINGS

John 3:19–21

Romans 13:11–14

1 John 1:5–7

Concluding Thoughts

Another young Hollywood star died recently. The news journalists reported that this individual had problems with addictions. We dislike being in the dark or feeling blind, whether this condition is spiritual, emotional, or physical. God understands this fear. He knows that we often feel lost or disoriented. We think personal success will fill the sense of dissatisfaction in our hearts. It never works. Jesus has come to be our light. He will lead us out of our bleak situations. He offers a sense of purpose and a life of righteousness. He creates order out of our personal disorder and brings structure to our chaotic lives. His direction and enlightenment offer real inner peace and give us hope for our future.

Chapter 4

Our Perfect High Priest

KEY SCRIPTURE

"Therefore, since we have a great high priest who has gone through the heavens, Jesus the Son of God, let us hold firmly to the faith we profess."

Hebrews 4:14

Several times I have been asked to testify on behalf of a client. It usually is a situation when his or her word needs more support or evidence. These individuals have provided references and proof of being truthful, but the legal system wants a professional opinion. My clients are usually scared and desperate, since their lives will be profoundly affected by the court's decision. I find such situations uncomfortable. Will I provide accurate and helpful answers? Will I represent and advocate well for my client?

Thankfully, most of us will not need such representation in a legal battle. In fact, we rarely have an advocate in most of life circumstances. The need for an intercessor seems unusual. Or is it?

Have you ever thought about what it would be like to enter into the presence of God? Would you be scared or excited? I think it would be terrifying. There are many biblical passages that speak of the awesomeness of God. Moses asked to see God's glory, and God had to place his hand over Moses' eyes to keep Moses protected from his overwhelming, amazing presence. Moses was only allowed to see God's back (Exodus 33:18–23). I am reminded of the story of the destruction of Sodom and Gomorrah. God's judgment was so powerful that one could not look upon it without being destroyed. Lot's wife, through her disobedience, discovered this and was turned into a pillar of salt with one backward glance (Genesis 19:23–26). Jesus tells us that no one has seen God (John 1:18).

God is *Holy* and I am not. He is infinite, and I am very frail and finite. He is the Creator, and I only duplicate in some form what has already been done a thousand times before. God made, knows the names of, and calls out each star (Isaiah 40:26). I am lucky if I can recognize a few constellations. I think I would be physically undone if I were to enter the throne room of God.

How, then, can any of us take our requests and petitions to God? How can we hope to have a relationship with him? During the time of Moses, God set up a system of Levitical priests to offer sacrifices and make petitions on behalf of God's people, the Israelites. It was through this system that prayers and petitions could be made directly to God. But it was temporary, complex, and cumbersome. Jesus instituted a new way to enter the throne room of God. He offered himself as our new high priest and devised a perfect system. His was not temporary. It is because of Jesus, our perfect High Priest, that we now can confidently enter into God's presence.

OPENING QUESTIONS

Have you used an advocate before, such as an attorney, a therapist, or a medical case manager? How well were you represented?

When you pray, have you ever thought about the fact that you are entering God's presence to talk to him?

Have you felt the need for a priest to intercede on your behalf to God? Why or why not?

MEDITATION EXERCISE

Let's use the practice of *Lectio divina* this week. You may want to use the Scripture verses Hebrews 10:19–22 as a focus. Just as a reminder, read these verses aloud, slowly, and with close attention. After the reading, ask God to speak to you through this passage. Re-read the passage aloud. Listen and journal what you hear God saying to you through these Scripture verses. You may want to use the same passage several days in a row.

"Understand"

Stay Jeremy Camp

"You Are My Refuge"

In That Day: Praise Band 10 Maranatha! Praise Band

"Come Be Who You Are"

City on a Hill: A Gathering Sara Groves

"My Glorious"

Glo Delirious?

Jesus, Our High Priest

KEY READING

Therefore, since we have a great high priest who has ascended into heaven, Jesus the Son of God, let us hold firmly to the faith we profess. For we do not have a high priest who is unable to empathize with our weaknesses, but we have one who has been tempted in every way, just as we are—yet he did not sin.

Hebrews 4:14–15

Marital therapy is common in most clinical practices. Couples seek help when they have hit an impasse on an important issue or when their marriages have become tense and conflict-ridden. Spouses commonly discuss disagreements in treatment. They are angry and hurt and need a professional to listen and represent both sides of the issue. Sometimes the conflict isn't solved within the time limits of a session, and the couple leaves the office without closure. Therapists establish guidelines to help in such situations. Each spouse is not to discuss his or her side of the disagreement until both parties return to the next session. This rule exists because the counselor cannot go home with the couple. The husband and wife lack an intercessor until they return to the next treatment session.

We do not have this problem with Jesus. His intercession is never-ending. Many of us go through each day having conversations with God. Prayer seems completely natural. We don't go through any motions to prepare ourselves for prayer time. Many of us don't kneel or bow. We usually don't fast from certain foods or put on special clothes. Some of us may act like entering into the presence of God is a casual thing, nothing out of the ordinary or frightening about it. But this misses something critical. We are only able to have this open, easy, almost casual prayer life with God because of what Jesus has done and is currently doing on our behalf. He is our High Priest who, right now, is on the right hand of God interceding for us.

Richard Foster writes,

> If the key is prayer, the door is Jesus Christ. How good of God to provide us a way into his heart. He knows that we are stiff-necked and hard-hearted, so he has provided a means of entrance. Jesus, the Christ, lived a perfect life, died in our place, and rose victorious over the dark powers so that we might live through him. This is wonderfully good news. No longer do we have to stand outside, barred from nearness to God by our rebellion. We may now enter through the door of God's grace and mercy in Jesus Christ.[7]

I enter my time of prayer very easily, without much thought or preparation. Until now, I have not stopped to think about the continuous intercessory work Jesus has done to make this so simple.

※ Have you been aware of your need for a priest?

※ How does having a better understanding of the role of Jesus, our priest, change your thoughts about prayer time?

PRAYER

Dear Jesus, thank you for being my High Priest. Thank you for mediating for me in the throne room of heaven. Because of you, I can enter the Most Holy Place with confidence.

OPTIONAL READINGS

Numbers 1:44–54

Leviticus 16:1–34

Jesus, Our Perfect Priest

KEY READING

But when Christ came as high priest of the good things that are now already here, he went through the greater and more perfect tabernacle that is not made with human hands, that is to say, is not a part of this creation. He did not enter by means of the blood of goats and calves; but he entered the Most Holy Place once for all by his own blood, thus obtaining eternal redemption. The blood of goats and bulls and the ashes of a heifer sprinkled on those who are ceremonially unclean sanctify them so that they are outwardly clean. How much more, then, will the blood of Christ, who through the eternal Spirit offered himself unblemished to God, cleanse our consciences from acts that lead to death, so that we may serve the living God!

For this reason Christ is the mediator of a new covenant, that those who are called may receive the promised eternal inheritance—now that he has died as a ransom to set them free from the sins committed under the first covenant.

Hebrews 9:11–15

God established with Moses the system of priests, which provided a way for the people to be cleansed from their sins. This required a building or earthly sanctuary to be set up as a place of offering and a place to meet with God. Priests could enter into the outer room to carry on their ministry. The high priest entered the most holy place only once a year, after he made blood sacrifices to cover his own sin. Once inside, the high priest offered blood sacrifices on behalf of the people to cleanse them from their sins. But this was a temporary measure. Despite the rules and regulations to help God's people maintain purity, their hearts did not change—their propensity to sin continued. So, sacrifices were continually needed to provide atonement for their sinfulness.

Jesus provided a different way. He brought about a perfect way with a perfect sanctuary. His sanctuary is not manmade and not of this physical realm. This sanctuary is the throne room of God Almighty, where Jesus sits at God's right hand. Jesus does not come only on a yearly basis, but rather serves there continually on our behalf. He does not need the blood of animals to cover his sin. Jesus is without sin, "blemish-free." He does not come into this tabernacle to offer animal sacrifices, but rather offers his own blood to cover our sins. This sacrifice does not only cleanse us from all our past sins, it covers all our sins: past, present and future. It is a *once* and *for all* sacrifice. This blood does even more. It provides internal cleansing of our consciences and changes our hearts. Jesus' way is open to all, not just to the tribes of Israel. It is available to anyone who accepts this wonderful, cleansing gift.

꙳ Have you ever found yourself trying to earn atonement or righteousness by your efforts, such as being a good person or carefully following a certain set of rules? What was that like?

꙳ How does this affect you to know that you are set free from a system of sacrifices because of Jesus' perfect priesthood?

꙳ How does it change your life to be set free of your sinfulness, once and for all?

PRAYER

Dear Jesus, thank you for setting me free from the old system of laws and regulations. Thank you for setting me free from my sinfulness. Let this reality sink deep into my heart. Keep me from any type of legalism on which I think I have to earn my own righteousness.

OPTIONAL READINGS

Hebrews 8:1–2; 10:1–10

Jesus, Our Priest with Humanity

KEY READING

For we do not have a high priest who is unable to empathize with our weaknesses, but we have one who has been tempted in every way, just as we are—yet he did not sin. Let us then approach God's throne of grace with confidence, so that we may receive mercy and find grace to help us in our time of need.

Hebrews 4:14–16

Have you ever wondered if another person understands what it is like to be tempted by your struggles? What it is like to be inside your skin and to face the same battles continuously? Maybe you have a habit or an addiction that you have tried to break. The author of Hebrews says that Jesus understands. He does not have just empathy and compassion for you. His understanding goes much deeper. Jesus was "tempted in every way" (Hebrews 4:15). Can you imagine being tempted in every possible way? There are some sins that may be more attractive to you whereas other temptations just don't appeal as much. But Jesus faced every sin. It's common to think of Jesus as someone who didn't experience any temptation, let alone all of them. Despite being without sin, Jesus understands your plight.

Jesus shares in our humanity. Just as he is God, he is also human. He shares our weaknesses. He understands what it feels like to be alone, cold, and hungry. He experienced rejection and hatred. He frequently had people despise him so much they plotted his death. He knows what it is to be the outcast. He is our brother. And because of this shared humanity, he is an understanding, merciful priest who sympathizes with all of our challenges and weaknesses. He gets it. We can be bold when we come to him with our fears, failures, and struggles. Jesus gets it.

❊ Do you feel a freedom to come to Jesus about any concern or failure? Or do you find yourself feeling embarrassed and ashamed about some area of your life?

❊ How does it change things to know that Jesus faced every temptation?

❊ What difficult areas of your life do you need to talk to Jesus about today?

PRAYER

Dear Jesus, thank you for being my merciful High Priest. I am very grateful that you intimately understand all my weaknesses and struggles. Thank you for being sympathetic to my challenges. Please meet me today in my current difficulty and bring victory.

OPTIONAL READINGS

Matthew 4:1–11

Hebrews 2:11–18

Jesus, Our Forever Priest

KEY READING

Therefore, I urge you, brothers and sisters, in view of God's mercy, to offer your bodies as a living sacrifice, holy and pleasing to God—this is your true and proper worship.

Romans 12:1

I find it odd that God goes to the trouble of setting up the Levitical system of priests only to tell us in Hebrews that Jesus isn't of this type of priesthood. Instead, he is of the order of Melchizedek (Hebrews 7:11). Why does God do that? Hebrews tells us that Jesus has come to bring us a "new" type of priesthood. Not just a better way, but a *perfect* way. This priesthood is not based on regulations or ancestry but on the power of Jesus' "indestructible life" (Hebrews 7:16). Talk about giving me confidence when I long to approach God! I can have a sense of safety and boldness when I bring my struggles, my concerns, and my joys to God.

But it does not stop there. Jesus' priesthood extends to you and me. Our obedient walk with God is the practice in this new order of priesthood. Our daily sacrifice is ourselves. When we love others, praise and thank God, and perform acts of service and kindness, we are like the priests of old going before God to worship and serve him. This pleases God. Just like those priests, we also have a ministry. Like them, we can intercede on the behalf of others. As Paul puts it, we are "Christ's ambassadors" with a "ministry of reconciliation" (2 Corinthians 5:19–20). We are to extend God's love and mercy to others. "You are a letter from Christ" that speaks of God's love to those who don't know him (2 Corinthians 3:3). And as we extend this love, it is like the sweet aroma of burnt sacrifice to God.

🌿 Have you ever considered yourself a priest?

🌿 How does this shift your spiritual perspective to know that you have a "ministry of reconciliation?"

🌿 How will being an "ambassador" of Jesus change what you do today?

PRAYER

Dear Jesus, thank you for bringing about a perfect priesthood. I have not always been faithful in being your ambassador. Embolden me to be confident and faithful in extending your love to others. Let me be deeply aware of how much this pleases you.

OPTIONAL READINGS

Genesis 14:17–20

Hebrews 7:1–28; 13:15–16

Concluding Thoughts

Advocacy isn't a common practice unless one's legal status is in question. Most people don't think of their need for an intermediary to act on their behalf. Each person, once legally an adult, is able to sign medical documents, write monetary checks, and come and go from work, school, and medical facilities. This freedom is possible because every adult person is his or her own legal representative.

Because of the ease to represent ourselves on a daily basis, it is easy to forget that this freedom doesn't extend to our relationship with God. We only are able to approach God with our prayers and petitions because of Jesus' constant and consistent intercession. At this very moment, Jesus is in God's throne room advocating for us. His intercession makes it easy for us. Let us not forget Jesus' role and take this wonderful access to God for granted.

Chapter 5

Our Teacher

KEY SCRIPTURE

*"Tax collectors also came to be baptized. 'Teacher,' they asked,
'what should we do?'"*

Luke 3:12

Education is a regular part of my counseling. I teach clients about
mental disorders and treatment options. Clients learn about their
current daily coping strategies and how to use more effective relationship
skills. Teaching occurs in many settings. For example, pastors teach the
Bible from the pulpit, and nurses instruct on good health practices at
medical clinics. Teacher relationships are very common.

As I thought about Jesus as our teacher, I realized that most of us
have strong associations with the word "teacher." Some of us have had
teachers believe in us and inspire us to greater achievements. Others
of us may have found our experiences with teachers to be discouraging.
Maybe you had a teacher who didn't listen to you or seem to care about
your struggles.

What was the association like with someone from Jesus' day? Who
was taught and what was that learning experience like? I was amazed

at the number of references in the New Testament to Jesus as a teacher. The association with Jesus as a teacher was strong. It is important that we understand what this reference meant so we can enter into a similar type of relationship with Jesus.

According to Ralph Gower, in his book *The New Manners and Customs of Bible Times,* Jewish boys started instruction at the age of six. Young boys attended a school called "house of the book" for their education. They sat in a semi-circle on the floor, facing their teacher. The teaching method was mostly comprised of rote memorization and recitation with only one textbook, the Taanach. This was also known as the Law, Prophets, and Writings, much of what comprises the Old Testament. Boys, age ten to fifteen, learned traditional and Jewish law. Only the best and the brightest received any further instruction; those students would go on to Jerusalem to one of the law schools. A bright young man would ask to be accepted as a disciple of a famous rabbi. If chosen, he would live with and learn from the rabbi. Paul had been a student in this type of Jewish educational system. His education was one of the finest. He was a Pharisee and a son of a Pharisee (Act 23:6).

This is a very different learning experience from our current classrooms. I find it interesting that many who sought Jesus identified him as rabbi or teacher. They viewed him as one who had answers. Do we view Jesus as our teacher? How would it change our relationship with him if we looked at him as someone who desires to increase our knowledge of God? Let's explore this relationship further and invite Jesus to teach us.

OPENING QUESTIONS

What have been your experiences with teachers?

Who was your favorite teacher? Why?

Who was your worst? Why?

Do you see Jesus as your Teacher? Why or why not?

MEDITATION EXERCISE

This week be on the lookout for what God may be saying to you. You might have a personal experience or a dream that speaks to you. What might God be teaching you? Record what you hear God saying to you in your journal or share it with someone else.

"Come to Me"

Jill Paquette Jill Paquette

"Thy Word"

Celtic Praise Eden's Bridge

"Be Thou My Vision"

The Breaking of the Dawn Fernando Ortega

Being a Disciple of Jesus

KEY READING

As Jesus was walking beside the Sea of Galilee, he saw two brothers, Simon called Peter and his brother Andrew. They were casting a net into the lake, for they were fishermen. "Come, follow me," Jesus said, "and I will send you out to fish for people." At once they left their nets and followed him.

Going on from there, he saw two other brothers, James son of Zebedee and his brother John. They were in a boat with their father Zebedee, preparing their nets. Jesus called them, and immediately they left the boat and their father and followed him.

Matthew 4:18–22

Obtaining a higher education beyond childhood was something that few men achieved during Jesus' day. Young men would identify a particular doctrine within the Jewish community and ask to become a disciple of the teacher or rabbi of this doctrine. Only a select few were chosen. These men lived with their rabbi in order to learn from him. Paul drew our attention to this when he described his own education. He pointed out that he was "circumcised on the eighth day, of the people of Israel, of the tribe of Benjamin, a Hebrew of Hebrews; in regard to the law, a Pharisee; as for zeal, persecuting the church; as for legalistic righteousness, faultless" (Philippians 3:5–6). He was one of the select individuals accepted for further training by a rabbi (see Galatians 1:14). This was a difficult achievement and, in some circles, would have given Paul prestige.

Jesus came along and turned the whole system upside down. Instead of bright young men seeking his approval to become one of his disciples, Jesus went hunting for his own disciples. He didn't seek them from places of religious education. He walked along the lake, saw a couple of fishermen, and invited them to be his disciples. Who were these men whom Jesus would call to be his disciples? Have you ever looked at the roster of Jesus' disciples? Five of them were former fishermen, and one was a tax collector. The rest of them had unknown occupations. This was shocking. Jesus was revolutionary as a teacher.

His outrageous behavior did not stop with inviting unlearned men and known sinners to be his disciples. He also let women learn from him. Take the Samaritan woman at the well. He met her and knew she was of the "wrong sort," by culture and by her behavior, yet he still engaged her in a spiritual discussion. He let Mary join a group of men he was instructing. She boldly sat at his feet, like one of the young pupils at the "house of the book." Martha chastised him for encouraging this behavior, but Jesus told Martha that Mary has chosen wisely (Luke 10:38–42).

In Jesus' day, most of us would not have qualified for a higher education since we are not bright enough or are not of the right gender. Did this change the way Jesus related to those around him? Did he only relate to the male gender and, then, only to the brightest of the men around him? Who sat at Jesus' feet for learning, and who did he call to be his disciples? Jesus broke all the rules. No one was exempt from his teachings. Jesus stills offers himself as a teacher to *all* of us. Are we willing to be his pupils?

❦ Have you thought of Jesus as a teacher?

What comes to your mind when you consider this type of relationship with Jesus?

Have you let some obstacle (like intelligence or history) get in the way of learning from Jesus?

PRAYER

Dear Jesus, thank you for being my Teacher. This might be a foreign way to think of you. Help me to be open to the idea of being your disciple. I want to learn from you.

OPTIONAL READINGS

Mark 4:1–2

Luke 4:31–37; 10:38–42

Jesus' Words Are Sweeter than Honey

KEY READING

Teach me, Lord, the way of your decrees,
  that I may follow it to the end.
Give me understanding, so that I may keep your law
  and obey it with all my heart.
Direct me in the path of your commands,
  for there I find delight.
I have not departed from your laws,
  for you yourself have taught me.
How sweet are your words to my taste,
  sweeter than honey to my mouth!
I gain understanding from your precepts;
  therefore I hate every wrong path.
Your word is a lamp to my feet,
  and a light for my path.

Psalm 119:33–35, 102–105

The references to the word of God being sweeter than honey strikes me as odd. How does one "taste" knowledge? Ralph Gower, in his book *The New Manners and Customs of Bible Times*, explains these references.[9] When a boy went for his education in Jesus' day, he started school before daylight. After a period of instruction, this child would be taken to the teacher's home for breakfast. There he received cakes with the letters of the law written on them. What a wonderful way to learn the letters of the law. The student would associate the sweetness of the cakes with the alphabet.

Later, this student would learn by using slates, much in the same way as children in the colonial days of the United States used slates. They didn't have access to chalk, like our pioneer students. Instead, the slates were coated with honey and each boy used his pen to trace letters in the honey. Gower commented that boys would occasionally lick the nib of their pens as they worked. God tells us that his words are sweeter than the honey those boys enjoyed.

Throughout the New Testament Gospels, we read of how Jesus drew crowds of people and taught them. His most studied sermon is often called "The Beatitudes." In this teaching he told the crowd that he came to fulfill the Laws and the Prophets. He taught not just practices of the law, or rules for behavior, but what brought changes in one's heart. Prior to Jesus' teachings, one's righteousness was measured by the degree of keeping the law perfectly. Jesus went beyond this teaching to the purpose of the law: to love one another. Paul, in Romans 13:10, wrote it this way: "Love does no harm to its neighbor. Therefore love is the fulfillment of the law." What sweetness there is to Jesus' words. We can delight in obeying the law of God since this obedience results in us living well with God and each other. Jesus' words are sweeter than honey.

❦ Have you associated obedience with legalism?

❦ What differentiates the two?

❦ Have you experienced "sweetness" in Jesus' words? How?

PRAYER

Dear Jesus, thank you for fulfilling the Law and the prophets. Thank you for not leading me into legalistic behavior but rather into showing greater love for one another. Let your words become even sweeter to me as I gain more knowledge of you.

OPTIONAL READINGS

Psalm 19:9–10

Matthew 5:17–20

Jesus Increases Our Knowledge of God

KEY READING

The Son is the image of the invisible God, the firstborn over all creation. For in him all things were created: things in heaven and on earth, visible and invisible, whether thrones or powers or rulers or authorities; all things have been created through him and for him. He is before all things, and in him all things hold together. And he is the head of the body, the church; he is the beginning and the firstborn from among the dead, so that in everything he might have the supremacy. For God was pleased to have all his fullness dwell in him, and through him to reconcile to himself all things, whether things on earth or things in heaven, by making peace through his blood, shed on the cross.

Colossians 1:14b–20

Having a properly defined personal goal is critical in one's search for self-fulfillment. This comes up in counseling when I ask parents what is their primary objective in rearing children. Happiness? Being successful? Becoming responsible adults? Often a misdirected goal is the source of problems at home. For example, parents who want happy children often have a hard time saying "no" and setting appropriate limits. These children can become selfish or rebellious. Without well-defined goals in life to aim toward, it is easy to miss the mark. So, what is your purpose? What do you live for?

Alfred Edersheim, in his book *Sketches of Jewish Social Life*, tells us in Jesus' day, the Jewish individual's focus was to increase his knowledge of God. Everything was centered on this desire. He points out that even science was submerged in theology. "To the pious Jew... the knowledge of God was everything; and to prepare for or impart that knowledge was the sum total, the sole object of his education."[10]

Jesus is the fulfillment of this desire. Paul tells us that God was "pleased to have all his fullness dwell in him" (Colossians 1:19). Jesus is the "fullness" of God. The word comes from the Greek root word "pleroo," which means filled up or complete. In other words, you can know God by knowing Jesus. The completeness of God is found in Jesus.

This brings me back to my original question: what is the point of your life? Jesus wants you to know and serve God. He desires God to be the "pleasure" of your life. The Jewish people of Bible times had it right, with this change: instead of focusing your education on learning the law in order to know God, you are to focus on Jesus to know God.

❧ Based upon your activities and mental preoccupations, what would you say is the purpose of your life?

❧ Does it line up with your desired goal?

❧ What changes do you need to make so your lifestyle will match your desired purpose?

PRAYER

Dear Jesus, thank you for being the "fullness of God." I need help with my purpose in life. Increase my desire to know you more so that it will become the whole point of my life.

OPTIONAL READINGS

John 3:1–21; 13:1–17

Following Means Obeying Our Teacher

KEY READING

We know that we have come to know him if we keep his commands. Whoever says, "I know him," but does not do what he commands is a liar, and the truth is not in that person. But if anyone obeys his word, love for God is truly made complete in them. This is how we know we are in him: Whoever claims to live in him must live as Jesus did.

1 John 2:3–6

When I started my counseling practice, I had the idea, maybe a hope, that insight would lead to psychological and behavioral changes. I discovered that this isn't true. I can still remember the particular patient I was counseling when I discovered this reality. She had a troubling behavior she wanted to stop. We worked for weeks trying to uncover the hidden motives and conflicts that were driving her. Despite gaining several significant insights, her problem continued. I came to the sad conclusion that change did not come from psychological understanding. Despite knowing more of her hidden motives, she was still a prisoner to her habit. Is this a biblical concept or an American trait?

The Bible says that this lack of change from psychological insight is a cultural issue. According to Scripture, to hear or know is to be transformed. Why in this Western culture have we separated the two? I recently asked one of my teenagers to do a chore. He told me, "Sure," but continued with his activity. Had he heard me? I couldn't tell. Jesus would have said that he didn't hear me since he didn't obey me. This is what he means by saying repeatedly, "He who has ears, let him hear." Understanding or knowing brings change or healing. To grasp the words of Jesus is to be touched and transformed by them. If we are not changed, then we never really understood them. This makes me uncomfortable. It forces me to get honest. What part of my life is still trapped by sin? What truth am I not understanding that leaves me broken?

🌿 What do you think of the biblical concept that to hear a truth is to be changed by it?

🌿 Have you found understanding God's word brings change to your life?

🌿 Why do you think you aren't changed every time by every new truth you learn?

🌿 Name one place in your life where you are struggling with sin. What truth do you not understand?

PRAYER

Dear Jesus, I want to be transformed by truth. Show me what I do not understand so I will no longer be a prisoner to that sin. Thank you for setting me free.

OPTIONAL READINGS

Matthew 13:9, 13–15, 43

Luke 11:39–40

Concluding Thoughts

In Jesus' day only the brightest young men were considered to become a rabbi's students. Once a boy was accepted as a pupil, he would go wherever the rabbi went and do exactly what the rabbi did. He would adopt the rabbi's behavior, attitudes, and opinions.

Jesus turned this whole process upside down. He didn't wait for candidates to seek him for training. He approached unlikely men to be his students. He did not reject potential disciples due to their lack of training or intelligence. Instead, he invited the most implausible individuals to be his students.

This invitation is still open to us. Jesus' request to follow him continues today. This call has the same requirements for us as it did for the first group of disciples. If we are true followers of Jesus, then we, too, will adopt his mannerisms and his attitudes. We will not just be hearers of his words, but also doers. His teachings are sweet and feed our souls. Our lives will have real purpose and meaning if we take his call seriously.

Chapter 6

The Good Shepherd

KEY SCRIPTURE

"I am the good shepherd. The good shepherd lays down his life for the sheep."

John 10:11

My mom and I owned a flock of sheep for several years. It was quite a learning experience for me. I was shocked to find out how vulnerable sheep are. They are more than dumb; they are downright stupid. One of our older lambs got caught in the wooden feeder and couldn't get itself out. After several hours of being trapped, it was growing weak and would have eventually given up and died had it not been found.

Sheep run in groups, are silly, easily scared, and under constant threat from predators. We had a donkey live with our flock of sheep to help keep wild dogs and coyotes away. We also kept the flock close to our home so that we could hear the animals at night if they got into trouble. This wasn't the case during psalmist David's time. Instead, a family member or a hired hand would stay out in the fields and live with the flock. Their presence acted as a deterrent to many threats and gave the shepherd the opportunity to chase away any attacking predators.

Sheep need regular care. One cannot own a flock of sheep and trust the sheep to care for most of their own needs. They are not independent like a housecat who just looks for regular water and feeding. In addition to needing food, clean pastures, and water, sheep require annual shearing, hoof trimming, and help with birthing. They can wander off and fall into holes. They are vulnerable to getting lost or trapped.

Throughout the Bible humanity is referred to as being like sheep. I am not sure how I feel about this. Am I vulnerable? Do I need constant attention and care? Do I make silly and stupid decisions? Do I give up easily after I have made a mess and gotten myself caught and trapped? Can I get lost? Unfortunately, these descriptions are too often true. Thankfully, Jesus is my good shepherd.

How is my therapeutic relationship with my clients like the shepherd's relationship with his sheep? Each individual who seeks counseling is looking for guidance similar to a lost sheep needing help getting home. As a counselor, I need to be careful not to create the same kind of dependence for me that sheep have for their shepherd. I am proceeding in a risky direction if I take charge of my clients' lives and give too many specific directions. This is too much power and responsibility to assume. As a clinician, I need to be careful not to encourage a great deal of dependency, since one of my primary objectives is to help clients to no longer need treatment. Fortunately, these kinds of restrictions are not needed with Jesus. He is the ultimate therapist and the good shepherd. We are encouraged to depend on him for all of our needs. He looks out for us. He desires to direct our lives since each of us matters to him.

OPENING QUESTIONS

What comes to your mind when you think of sheep?

How does it feel to have the Bible compare you to sheep?

Do you see Jesus as your shepherd? What does this mean to you?

Let's use Psalm 23 as the focus for *Lectio divina* this week. As you listen to yourself read these verses, what stands out to you? How is God using this emphasis to speak to a specific situation in your life? Does the focus change from day to day? You may want to write in a journal what you learn from this week's exercise.

PLAYLIST

"The Ninety and Nine"

Carried Along Andrew Peterson

"Arise and Be Comforted"

A Grateful People Watermark

"Abide With Me"

Celtic Reflections on Hymns Eden's Bridge

"You Never Let Go"

Passion: Everything Glorious Matt Redman

Jesus, The Voice of the Shepherd

KEY READING

"I am the good shepherd; I know my sheep and my sheep know me—just as the Father knows me and I know the Father—and I lay down my life for the sheep. I have other sheep that are not of this sheep pen. I must bring them also. They too will listen to my voice, and there shall be one flock and one shepherd. The reason my Father loves me is that I lay down my life—only to take it up again. No one takes it from me, but I lay it down of my own accord. I have authority to lay it down and authority to take it up again. This command I received from my Father."

John 10:14–18

Around lambing time our sheep farm often would have visitors. Families with small children loved to see and hold the baby lambs. Since sheep are easily skittish and frightened, one of our rules for visitors was that they seldom speak and only softly. It was amazing that our sheep knew who the strangers were and who the shepherds were by our voices. Strangers brought foreignness and fear, but the shepherds brought consistency and trust.

Our sheep's trust was developed by my parents' daily care for them. They talked to them while completing chores. The sheep grew to know and trust the voices of my parents through the constant contact. Eventually, the sound of my parents' voices meant food was coming, and the sheep would run to the fences to meet them. The presence of strangers did not evoke trust for our sheep. Often they ran to the farthest corners of the pasture at the mere sound or sense of a stranger.

We, like the sheep, come to know the voice of our Shepherd. We can only do this with consistent contact with Jesus. Do we spend regular time with him? He regularly comes to us. In fact, he is always with us. He loves to hear our prayers, to soothe us when we are afraid, and to comfort us when we are sad. Just like sheep, through this daily contact, we grow to know the trustworthiness of our Shepherd. We learn of his reliability, his sensitivity, his mercy, and his love. But this only occurs when we seek him on a regular basis so that he becomes very familiar and known to us.

❧ How is your daily spiritual life? Do you spend time with Jesus on a regular basis? If not, what gets in the way of that?

❧ Have you found that the more time you spend with Jesus the better you are at distinguishing truth from the world's lies?

PRAYER

Dear Jesus, thank you for being my Good Shepherd. I realize that I come to know your voice by spending time with you. Help me to identify ways that I sabotage my time with you. Empower me to change those destructive practices so that my relationship with you becomes even stronger.

OPTIONAL READINGS

Psalm 23

John 10:1–6, 25–30

Jesus, the Shepherd Who Knows Our Names

KEY READING

Now the tax collectors and sinners were all gathering around to hear Jesus. But the Pharisees and the teachers of the law muttered, "This man welcomes sinners and eats with them."

Then Jesus told them this parable: "Suppose one of you has a hundred sheep and loses one of them. Doesn't he leave the ninety-nine in the open country and go after the lost sheep until he finds it? And when he finds it, he joyfully puts it on his shoulders and goes home. Then he calls his friends and neighbors together and says, 'Rejoice with me; I have found my lost sheep.' I tell you that in the same way there will be more rejoicing in heaven over one sinner who repents than over ninety-nine righteous persons who do not need to repent."

Luke 15:1–7

Sheep recognize the voice of their shepherd, and the shepherd knows the names of his sheep. There is mutuality to the relationship. I have been a part of large organizations, institutions with hundreds of members. During my experiences I have often wondered if the leadership would recognize me as a member and know my name. I felt small, insignificant, and invisible. I was just a piece of the whole, not significant except for what I added to the whole. Or so I thought. Have you ever wondered about this when it comes to Jesus? If he is listening to all the prayers from all those who are praying around the world, can he recognize yours? Jesus tells us that he can.

Jesus is the shepherd who knows the names and needs of every sheep. During biblical times, shepherds would bring sheep inside a protected area at night. As the sheep walked through the gate, the shepherd would stand at the gate and count each sheep as it passed. He not only knew how many he cared for, but also if any were missing. As they passed by him, he would take note of their physical condition. Which had been sick or injured? Which looked hungry and malnourished?

Goats would also run with sheep. It made sense since they also required grazing. At times the shepherd would separate the flock into only sheep and only goats. The shepherd would use his staff at these times to separate each group. While under his care nothing missed the gaze of the shepherd. He knew his sheep.

Jesus has this same type of relationship with each of us. We are under his care. He knows when we are tired, sick, injured, or lost. He knows whether we are goats (see Matthew 25:31–46) or sheep. You and I matter to him. He is personally invested in our well-being. Nothing about our lives is invisible to him. Jesus is our shepherd, and he knows our names.

🜲 Have you been a part of a large institution? What was your experience as a part of such an organization?

🜲 Tell about a time when you felt the personal ministration of Jesus during something difficult?

❦ What obstacles make it hard to feel confident that Jesus is personally invested in you?

PRAYER

Dear Jesus, thank you for being my Good Shepherd. I am aware that you know me and know my struggles. You are invested in every detail of my life, just as the shepherd is invested in his sheep's well-being. Please help me to remember this when doubt and fear overwhelm me.

OPTIONAL READINGS

Ezekiel 34:11–16

Matthew 25:31–46

John 10:14–16

Jesus, Our Gate

KEY READING

"The man who enters by the gate is the shepherd of his sheep. The watchman opens the gate for him, and the sheep listen to his voice. He calls his own sheep by name and leads them out. When he has brought out all his own, he goes on ahead of them, and his sheep follow him because they know his voice. But they will never follow a stranger; in fact, they will run away from him because they do not recognize a stranger's voice."

"I am the gate; whoever enters through me will be saved. He will come in and go out, and find pasture."

John 10:2–5, 9

Our sheep pen had a large metal gate that swung open and shut. We chose one that was large enough to accommodate a tractor and wagon so that we could haul in hay and feed. Shepherds during Jesus' time did not have such luxury. Due to the dry conditions, shepherds would roam large areas with their flock to search for good pasture and clean streams of water. They may have ended up far from home base and needing a makeshift shelter at night for protection. Brad Young, in his book *Jesus the Jewish Theologian*, describes this nightly process.[11] The shepherd would find a natural barrier, like a cave or the side of a hill, and then gather stones to build a crude fence in order to create a temporary holding pen for the night. The stone wall would form a semi-circle, leaving an opening for the sheep to enter.

After the sheep were gathered in for the night, the shepherd would lie across the opening using himself as a "human gate" for the fence. There he would sleep for the night, creating a barrier to keep the sheep in and the predators out. After a night of being penned in, the sheep would be anxious to get out in the morning. Besides leaving the gate open, the shepherd would knock out a section of the piled-up stones so the sheep could "break out" (see Micah 2:13). The sheep would rush toward this opening, breaking down more of the makeshift fence as they pushed through.

Just as the shepherds of old were the gates for their flocks of sheep, so is Jesus our gate. He creates a safe place for us and uses himself as its barrier. He determines when we need such close shelters and when it is time for us to graze. The only way we can benefit from such close care is to be in a true relationship with Jesus. We cannot have a "come and go" type of relationship with him. This means coming to terms with our constant need for him. It also means coming to terms with our "sheep-ness" and our state of vulnerability that requires such care. Jesus longs to be our gate, but we must submit to being his sheep.

❋ What comes to your mind when you picture a shepherd's nightly ritual of building temporary shelter for the sheep?

❋ What is your emotional reaction to the picture of Jesus as the gate?

❋ What part(s) do you hold back in your submission to Jesus' care?

PRAYER

Dear Jesus, thank you for being the gate for me. You use yourself to aid in my protection. I am grateful for such a sacrifice. You truly are my Good Shepherd.

OPTIONAL READINGS

Micah 2:13

Jesus, Our Shepherd

KEY READING

He tends his flock like a shepherd:
He gathers the lambs in his arms
and carries them close to his heart;
he gently leads those that have young.

Isaiah 40:11

What is most precious to you? Have you noticed the effort you put into its care and protection? I have seen some people go to great lengths to keep their favored possession in good repair. I have a neighbor who regularly washes and waxes his car. I thought the car looked clean before he started. Or maybe you have a preferred relationship. Do you work to stay in touch, sharing your day and observations with that individual? It is interesting to see where people put their time and energy. Some folks put a significant priority on acquiring and maintaining material possessions; others put energy into maintaining a certain level of achievement. Some people like to maintain a particular position of influence, whereas others work to achieve a certain level of physical fitness.

Where did Jesus place his emphasis and attention? He accumulated no wealth. He lacked position and power, and, in fact, was often hated and despised. He had no home or even a place to lay his head at night, except for the graciousness of others. Jesus put all of his energy into building relationships. Jesus was like the shepherds of old. He lived with, cared for, and risked his life for his sheep. He compared himself to a shepherd, but he didn't just use words. He lived it out, even to the point of laying down his life so you and I could be safe and free.

I believe the words used to describe Jesus as our shepherd are actual descriptors of the type of relationship he desires with us. He wants us to depend on him for our needs, even the everyday, ordinary ones. He seeks us when we get lost and deceived by worldly concerns and our own sinfulness. He longs to carry us on his shoulders, when we are weak, tired, and weary from life. He protects us so successfully that our eternal life is secure, if we depend on him. So the critical question comes down to this: is Jesus our shepherd? If so, do we daily depend on him for our needs? If not, why not?

❦ Define your relationship with Jesus as the Good Shepherd.

❦ Shepherds have a very personal relationship with their sheep.
   The sheep's life is utterly dependent on the faithfulness of the
   shepherd. Jesus likens himself to a shepherd. Have you accepted
   your sheep-likeness and grown in your need for Jesus?

❦ What gets in the way of your increasing dependence on him for your
   security and safety?

PRAYER

Dear Jesus, thank you for being my Good Shepherd. Forgive me for my independence and not depending on you for my daily needs. You long to care for me just as the shepherds of old cared for their sheep. Help me to grow in trust in this type of relationship with you.

OPTIONAL READINGS

Isaiah 43:2

Luke 15:3–6

John 10:1–18

Concluding Thoughts

Emotional attachment occurs in counseling. Too much dependency results in clients being unable to leave the therapeutic relationship, and too little dependency results in limited treatment progress. Therapists can guide and support clients, but should not be these individuals' only source of emotional sustenance. Jesus does not have this same limitation. The Bible says that we are sheep, needing constant and consistent care. Jesus wants to meet *all* of our needs. There is no risk of inappropriate reliance, since Jesus is completely trustworthy and this relationship is everlasting.

Sources

Introduction

[1]Winnicott, D.W. The use of an object, *International Journal of Psychoanalysis.* 50, (1969):711-716.

[2]Bruce Wampold. *The Great Psychotherapy Debate: Models, Methods, and Findings.* Lawrence Eribaum, 2001.

[3]Rogers, Carl. *Client-centered Therapy: Its Current Practice, Implications and Theory.* London: Constable, 1951.

Chapter 1: Emmanuel

[4]Harvey, Paul. "The Man and the Birds." Broadcast retrieved from *www.askthebirds.org/2009/03/paul-harvey.html.* (Accessed March 19, 2010.)

[5]"The Numbers Count: Mental Disorders in America." *National Institutes of Health. www.nimh.nih.gov/health/publications/the-numbers-count-mental-disorder-in-america/index.shtml.* (Accessed March 19, 2010.)

Chapter 3: The Light of God

[6]Foster, Richard J. *Celebration of Discipline: The Path to Spiritual Growth.* San Francisco: Harper Collins, 1992.

Chapter 4: Our Perfect High Priest

[7]Foster, Richard J. *Celebration of Discipline: The Path to Spiritual Growth.* San Francisco: Harper Collins, 1992.

Chapter 5: Our Teacher

[8]Gower, Ralph. *The New Manners and Customs of Bible Times.* Chicago: Moody Press, 1987.

[9]Gower, ibid.

[10]Edersheim, Alfred. *Sketches of Jewish Social Life.* Peabody, Massachusetts: Hendrickson Publishers, Inc., 1994.

Chapter 6: The Good Shepherd

[11]Young, Brad H. *Jesus, The Jewish Theologian.* Peabody, Massachusetts: Hendrickson Publishers, Inc., 1995.

NOTES

This is the first of two devotionals about Jesus' relationship with us. This book focused on how Jesus is the perfect or ultimate therapist. It explored roles he has with us that also occur in counseling practices. The next book, *Jesus, The Ultimate Therapist: Healing Without Limits*, goes even further. It will examine another six relationship types that Jesus has with each of us that a therapist can't have with clients because of the risk of harm and abuse to the client. For example, counselors should not lord over their clients and tell them what to do, yet Jesus, the King, safely can. They can't devote their entire day to counseling one client, yet Jesus, the Lamb, does. They shouldn't be their client's' friend or the treatment will be minimized and serve the needs of the therapist, but Jesus perfectly maintains this balance as Friend. Finally, they don't marry their clients, yet one day Jesus, the Bridegroom, will. Jesus can have all of these roles with us because he is without sin. He won't hurt us or corrupt the relationship with us for his gain. He is a type of therapist no human therapist can ever be. He is the *ultimate* therapist: one without limits.

For more information about how to contact the
author, please visit: *www.livinglife2thefullest.com*.

Made in the USA
Las Vegas, NV
05 March 2024

86725865R00066